INVESTIGATING SCIENCE CHALLENGES

Investigating

LIGHT

Richard Spilsbury

CRABTREE
PUBLISHING COMPANY
WWW.CRABTREEBOOKS.COM

CRABTREE
PUBLISHING COMPANY
WWW.CRABTREEBOOKS.COM

Author: Richard Spilsbury

Editors: Sarah Eason, Jennifer Sanderson, Petrice Custance, Reagan Miller

Proofreaders: Kris Hirschmann, Janine Deschenes

Indexer: Wendy Scavuzzo

Editorial director: Kathy Middleton

Design: Emma DeBanks

Cover design and additional artwork: Emma DeBanks

Photo research: Rachel Blount

Production coordinator and prepress technician: Tammy McGarr

Print coordinator: Katherine Berti

Consultant: David Hawksett

Produced for Crabtree Publishing Company by Calcium Creative

Photo Credits:

t=Top, tr=Top Right, tl=Top Left

Inside: Shutterstock: Agafe: pp. 16-17; Alexkich: pp. 10-11; Alphaspirit: pp. 26-27; Iness Arna: pp. 22-23; Jan van der Hoeven: p. 20c; Green Jo: pp. 20-21; Kasezo: p. 23c; Dmitry Naumov: pp. 8, 11c; Alena Ozerova: p. 6; Pixelrain: p. 15; Roland Shainidze: p. 1; Sunny Forest: pp. 4-5; Dennis van de Water: p. 5r; www.sandatlas.org: p. 7; Vlue: p. 14; Vovan: p. 9; Pavel Yavnik: p. 17r.

Cover: Tudor Photography.

Library and Archives Canada Cataloguing in Publication

Spilsbury, Richard, 1963-, author
    Investigating light / Richard Spilsbury.

(Investigating science challenges)
Includes index.
Issued in print and electronic formats.
ISBN 978-0-7787-4207-4 (hardcover).--
ISBN 978-0-7787-4294-4 (softcover).--
ISBN 978-1-4271-2011-3 (HTML)

    1. Light--Juvenile literature. 2. Light--Experiments--Juvenile literature. I. Title.

QC365.S64 2018   j535   C2017-907740-6
                                C2017-907741-4

Library of Congress Cataloging-in-Publication Data

Names: Spilsbury, Richard, 1963- author.
Title: Investigating light / Richard Spilsbury.
Description: New York, New York : Crabtree Publishing, [2018] | Series: Investigating science challenges | Includes index.
Identifiers: LCCN 2017059669 (print) | LCCN 2017060181 (ebook) | ISBN 9781427120113 (Electronic HTML) | ISBN 9780778742074 (reinforced library binding) | ISBN 9780778742944 (pbk.)
Subjects: LCSH: Light--Juvenile literature. | Light--Experiments--Juvenile literature.
Classification: LCC QC365 (ebook) | LCC QC365 .S6475 2018 (print) | DDC 535--dc23
LC record available at https://lccn.loc.gov/2017059669

Crabtree Publishing Company
www.crabtreebooks.com   1-800-387-7650

Printed in the U.S.A./022018/CG20171220

Published in Canada
Crabtree Publishing
616 Welland Ave.
St. Catharines, Ontario
L2M 5V6

Published in the United States
Crabtree Publishing
PMB 59051
350 Fifth Avenue, 59th Floor
New York, New York 10118

Published in the United Kingdom
Crabtree Publishing
Maritime House
Basin Road North, Hove
BN41 1WR

Published in Australia
Crabtree Publishing
3 Charles Street
Coburg North
VIC, 3058

CONTENTS

LIGHT UP

Light is essential to our lives. It allows us to see the world around us and be able to work, travel, and communicate with each other. Decorative holiday lights and bright fireworks bring us pleasure and excitement. We also rely on lights to keep us safe. Red lights mean danger or tell us to stop. Emergency vehicles use flashing lights to warn people to move out of the way when they are traveling fast.

What Are Sources of Light?

There are many different **sources** of light. Sources of light are objects that produce or release light. During the daytime, the Sun is the main natural source of light on Earth. This light source lights up half of Earth at one time from 93 million miles (150 million km) away. In the shade and at night, we use **artificial** sources of light, such as lamps and flashlights, so we can see.

The Sun is the world's most important natural source of light. Without sunshine, we would not have daylight or warmth.

4

Light Energy

Sunlight can move from the Sun all the way to Earth. Light from a lamp can spread out to brighten a room. This is because light is a form of **energy**. Energy is the power or ability to make things move, work, or happen. Energy can be transferred, or moved from one place to another. Light energy travels away from its source in straight lines.

Lighthouses are powerful sources of light. Their beams warn ships not to come too close to coastlines.

INVESTIGATE

Scientists **observe** the world around them and ask questions. They then plan and carry out **investigations** to find answers. In this book, you will carry out investigations to answer questions about light. On pages 28 and 29, you can find investigation tips, check your work, and read suggestions for other investigations you can try.

HEAT AND LIGHT

Most light comes from heat. When things such as a campfire, a stove, or a candle flame become hot, they produce light. Heat, like light, is a form of energy. The amazing thing about energy is that it can change from one form into another. It is never destroyed or created. When wood burns in a fire, some of the heat energy that is produced turns into light energy. That is why fires burn so brightly. A candle also gives off both light and heat energy, although in smaller amounts than a fire. Light from heat energy is called **incandescence**.

When wood is burned, some of the energy turns into heat energy and some turns into light energy.

The Sun

Like other stars, the Sun is made of hot gases. In the Sun's center, or core, these gases undergo **reactions** that create a lot of energy. This makes the Sun incredibly hot. The Sun is the closest star to our planet, so much of its heat and light energy reaches us. In fact, the Sun is so hot and it releases so much light energy that it glows white. The heat energy from the Sun turns into incandescent light energy. It is so bright, it will damage your eyes if you look directly at it.

Lava, the melted rock that spurts out of a volcano, is incredibly hot. It is so hot that it glows with a red light.

Other Forms of Light

There are some kinds of light that do not come from heat. Television and **fluorescent** lights work when special chemicals that release light are triggered by electricity. **Neon** lights, such as those that glow at night in some store signs, produce light when electricity passes through neon gas and causes it to give off light. **Bioluminescence** is light produced by living things. Some deep-sea animals, such as squid, produce light using **bacteria** or special **cells** inside their body. A firefly is an insect that mixes oxygen with chemicals inside its body to make a light with almost no heat at all.

SEEING THINGS

We can see the things around us only when there is light. When it is completely dark, we cannot see anything. We see light sources, such as lamps and flashlights, because they produce their own light. We see other objects when light **reflects** off them. When light reflects, it bounces off a surface. During the day, we can see trees, people, cars, and other objects because light bounces off them and enters our eyes.

Light must reflect off objects for us to see them. When we shine a lamp on a book, the light reflects off the pages so we can read them.

Reflecting and Absorbing Light

Reflections happen because light travels in a straight line as far as it can. When something gets in its way and it hits a solid object, such as a tree, light is either reflected or **absorbed**. If light is absorbed, it is soaked up. Black objects absorb light well and can convert light energy into heat. This is why dark surfaces feel warm in sunlight. If light reflects off a surface, it bounces off it and goes in a different direction, a little like the way a ball bounces when you throw it against the ground.

There is really no such thing as moonlight! The Moon is not a source of light like the Sun. We can see the Moon only because light from the Sun reflects off it.

How Do Eyes Work?

Light from a light source hits an object and reflects into our eyes. This reflected light enters the eye through the tiny black hole in the middle of the colored part of the eye. This is called the **pupil**. Then the light passes through a clear, curved part called the **lens**. The lens helps focus the light onto an area called the **retina** at the back of the eye. In the retina, the patterns of different colors and brightness of light are turned into messages that then travel to the brain. The brain processes the messages and tells you what you are looking at.

REFLECTIONS

Different materials and objects reflect light in different ways. Some surfaces reflect light very poorly, while others reflect light very well. When you shine a flashlight at a mirror or a smooth, shiny surface, the light reflects much better than it does when you shine the flashlight beam toward other surfaces, such as a wooden door. In a mirror, light can create a reflection, which is a mirror image of the things around it.

A curved mirror scatters light in different directions, which **distorts** reflections. This makes things look weird!

Scattering Light

When you look at a lake, you can see the reflection of the surrounding trees and buildings on the lake's surface. If the water is smooth, flat, and calm, the reflection will be clear. If the water is covered in ripples or waves, the light rays that hit the surface reflect in many different directions. The scattered light allows us to see objects around the lake, but it does not create clear images reflected in the water's surface.

10

Mirror Reflections

Mirrors are made from very smooth glass that is coated with a thin layer of metal. The smooth, shiny surface on a mirror is able to reflect most of the light that hits it. The rays are not scattered. Instead, they bounce back at the same **angle** they hit the mirror. That is why you can see yourself as clearly in a mirror as you look to other people. The image we see in a clear mirror is almost identical to the object that makes it. The only difference is that the image is reversed!

When light hits the bumpy surface of water like this, reflected light scatters in so many different directions that the reflections are blurry.

INVESTIGATE

Explore your surroundings to spot the surfaces that help you see your reflection most clearly. Do sidewalks or wooden benches reflect light well? On cars, do shiny paintwork, side mirrors, and windows reflect light better than tires and plastic interiors? Do you think driving would be safer if side mirrors were made from rubber or plastic? If so, why?

11

Let's Investigate
DIFFERENT REFLECTIONS

Light reflecting from surfaces helps us see them. Light also helps us see our reflection and lights up other things. Do you notice that the amount of reflection changes when you shine light on different surfaces? It changes because of differences in smoothness and color of the surfaces. Let's investigate how different surfaces reflect light.

You Will Need:
- An adult for help
- A pair of scissors
- A shoebox with a lid
- Tape
- Aluminum foil
- A small object such as a toy or pencil sharpener
- A small flashlight
- A piece of paper and a pen or a cell phone
- White paper
- Black paper

peephole

foil

Step 1: Ask an adult to help you cut a small peephole in the center of one of the short sides of the box. Cut a larger hole in one of the long sides. The larger hole should be just big enough to poke the flashlight through it.

Step 2: Use tape to attach some aluminum foil inside the box on the end of the box opposite your peephole. Place the small object inside the part of the box that is opposite the hole you cut for your flashlight. Put the lid on the box.

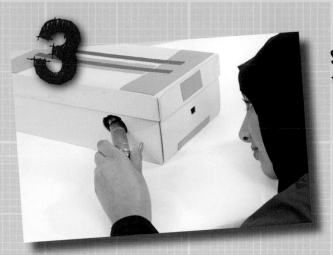

Step 3: Now put the head of the flashlight through the large hole and shine its beam at an angle toward the foil so it reflects onto the object. Look through the peephole. Is the object lit up by reflected light from the foil? Write down how well you can see the object by giving it a mark out of 10, or take a photo of it.

Step 4: Now repeat the experiment. But this time, replace the aluminum foil with a crumpled piece of aluminum foil, then white paper, then black paper. Remember what you have read about how light reflects differently from different surfaces. Which surface do you think will reflect the least amount of light, making it more difficult to see the object?

Science Challenge

Challenge Questions

- Which surface reflected light the best?
- Which surface absorbed light the best?
- Did the crumpled aluminum foil reflect light better or worse than smooth foil? Why?
- Why is it important to keep the flashlight at the same angle and place the objects in the same position?

MATERIALS AND LIGHT

Different things happen to light when it hits different materials. Different materials let in different amounts of light. An **opaque** material or object, such as a sheet of cardboard, blocks light from passing through. Light cannot pass through opaque objects such as stone walls, wooden doors, and thick fabric curtains. That is why we can use these things to block out any light in our rooms while we sleep.

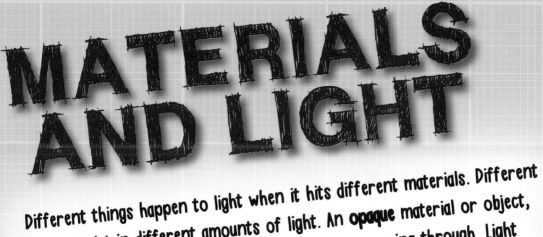

On a hot summer day, people sit under trees because the trees are opaque objects. They block the Sun, creating an area of cool shade.

What Materials Are Transparent?

Some materials are completely **transparent**. Light passes easily through them so they are see-through. Transparent materials include water, glass, and air. We make windows from glass to let light into our homes and to allow us to see outside. Much of the plastic packaging wrapped around foods and other products we buy is also transparent. The transparent covering keeps the items fresh and clean while allowing us to see what we are buying.

Why Are Translucent Materials Useful?

Translucent materials let some light pass through them, but not all of it. They also absorb some light or scatter it in all directions. That is why we can see through translucent materials, but not very clearly. Translucent materials are very useful in some types of glass and curtains. These let light into a room, such as a bathroom, but scatter the light so people outside cannot look inside. The **lenses** in sunglasses are also made from translucent materials. Wearers can see through the glasses, but colored tints and mirror coatings absorb or reflect bright sunlight to cut down its **glare**.

The lenses of sunglasses also have a translucent coating that absorbs and reflects harmful **ultraviolet** rays in sunlight that can damage our eyes.

SHADOWS

When objects block light, shadows form behind them, on the opposite side to where the light is shining. When you stand outside in the sunshine, your body blocks the sunlight and this can create a shadow the same shape as your body. Solid or opaque objects create dark shadows because no light passes through them at all. Translucent objects make very faint shadows. If you shine a flashlight through translucent material that is colored, such as a blue bottle or red tissue paper, you can make a colored shadow.

Shadows lengthen as the Sun gets lower in the sky and sets. These shadows look as though people have stretched out into giants.

Changing Shadows

Shadows can change size and shape. If an object is directly in front of a light source, the shadow it casts will be a similar shape and size to the object itself. When the light source is higher than an object, its shadow becomes shorter. When it is down low, the shadow gets longer. If the light source gets closer, an object's shadow gets bigger, but it becomes smaller when the light moves farther away. The shape of a shadow changes when the edge or side of the object facing the source of the light changes. That is why the shape of a shadow changes when you face toward a light and when you turn to the side.

16

Sun Shadows

During the day, the Sun seems to move across the sky. In fact, what is happening is that Earth is slowly rotating, or turning around, on its **axis**. This makes different edges or sides of objects face the Sun, so the sunlight hits the objects from different angles. This causes shadows to change shape.

It is fun making different shaped objects and looking at the shadows they form.

INVESTIGATE

Have you ever noticed that shadows are sometimes much bigger than the objects that make them, or that they are sometimes much smaller? What makes shadows change in size? Does an object make a bigger shadow on a wall when it is closer to a light source, such as a lamp on the other side of it, or farther away? Does it make any difference if the light source is brighter or dimmer? Try some tests to see if your ideas are right.

17

Let's Investigate
SHADOWS

Shadows form where light is blocked by an object. Have you seen how the size, shape, and clarity (how fuzzy or sharp the edges are) of your shadow can change? It depends partly on your position compared to the position of the light source. Let's investigate shadows by creating **silhouette** drawings.

You Will Need:
- A chair
- A room that can be made dark
- 2 friends
- Masking tape
- Large sheets of colored paper
- A tape measure
- A large, powerful flashlight
- A pencil

1

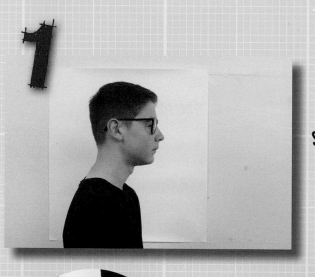

Step 1: Place the chair in front of a wall inside the room. Ask one friend to sit sideways on the chair. Tape a sheet of paper on the wall behind your friend's head and shoulders.

Step 2: Use the tape measure and masking tape to mark distances of 3, 6, 9, and 12 feet (1, 2, 3, and 4 m) from the chair. Check that the room is dark. Ask your friend to close his or her eyes. Ask the other friend to stand at the 6 feet (2 m) mark with the flashlight on and facing toward your seated friend.

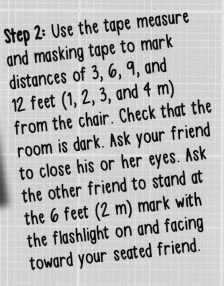

Step 3: Draw around your seated friend's head shadow to make a silhouette profile on the paper.

Step 4: Now repeat the experiment. This time, choose the distance mark that will give you the smallest shadow. Which one will make the largest silhouette? Remember what you have already learned about shadow sizes. Which distance mark do you think will make the sharpest silhouette?

- Which distance did you choose to draw the sharpest silhouette profile?
- Were shadows fuzzier or sharper when the flashlight was close to your seated friend? What caused these results?
- What was the difference in size between the smallest and biggest shadow head?
- If there was no difference in size, why do you think this was the case?
- Why must the person sitting on the chair stay in the position when you move the flashlight?

19

REFRACTION

When you look at a drinking straw in a glass of water from the side, something strange happens. At certain angles, it looks as though the straw is bent or broken. This happens because of **refraction**. Refraction is the way light bends when it passes through certain materials. When light passes through water, the water makes the light bend as you look at it. That is why a straw in a glass can look bent or broken.

Light always tries to travel in a straight or direct line, until something gets in its way. When light in the air hits water, this new substance makes light refract.

How Does Refraction Happen?

Refraction happens because light travels at different speeds through different materials. Light travels very quickly through air. That is why sunlight can travel all the way from the Sun to Earth in just eight minutes. Light moves more slowly through water. It slows down when it moves from air into water, so when it hits the edge of a water surface, it slows down and changes direction.

Light Tricks

The way light is refracted by water can also play tricks on us. When we look down into a pool or pond, the things in it can look closer or higher in the water than they really are. That is because the light reflecting off them is refracted as it leaves the water. Refraction can also make it look as though the water is shallower than it really is, so be careful when reaching into water for something below the surface.

The curved sides of this fishbowl act like a lens. They make the fish inside the water look bigger than it really is.

Looking at Lenses

The lenses in reading glasses and magnifying glasses are made from transparent, curved glass or plastic. The bulging shape of these **convex** lenses, which are wider in the middle than around the edges, refracts the light beams and makes objects looks bigger or closer to us. If you put a drop of water on transparent plastic over a newspaper, the words are magnified (made bigger) through the curved surface of the drop of water.

LIGHT SPECTRUM

Light is made up of a whole **spectrum**, or range, of colors. You have seen some of these colors when you look at a rainbow in the sky. Light can split into its different colors when it moves through certain materials, such as water or glass. As sunlight passes through tiny droplets of water in the air after a rainstorm, the light is reflected and refracted in a way that separates it into different colors that we can see.

A **prism** is a piece of glass with triangular ends. It refracts light and splits it into its different colors.

Playing with Prisms

Light moves slightly more slowly through glass than it does through water, so light refracts more as it hits and passes through glass. When light passes through a glass prism, some of the light is reflected and refracted more than other parts. Light leaving the prism spreads out into the band of colors called a spectrum. Colors range from red, which is bent least, to orange, yellow, green, blue, indigo, and all the way to violet, which is bent the most.

Diamonds and Light

A diamond is a rare, glasslike material that has many flat edges. When light hits a diamond, some of it reflects back, but some refracts into the center of the diamond and bounces around inside before it escapes. In this way, diamonds can also split light into different colors.

Seeing Colors

We see objects in different colors because of the way the individual colors within light are reflected or absorbed. For example, when light shines on a blue ball, most of the colors in that light are absorbed, so we do not see them. The blue colored part of sunlight reflects off the ball, so we see the ball as blue.

Raindrops can act like tiny prisms, refracting sunlight into different colors of the spectrum.

INVESTIGATE

You can create an artificial rainbow with a garden hose. Stand with your back to the Sun and adjust the hose to a fine spray. Try spraying the water at different angles. What happens? Rainbows are visible only to a person facing in the opposite direction to the Sun and at the precise angle at which drops of water reflect the light.

Let's Investigate RAINBOWS

By using a prism, we know that light is not white, but that it is made up of different colors. We can see those colors only in certain situations, such as when water or glass refract the light and split it into all its different colors, as in a rainbow. Let's investigate the colors of light by making a rainbow.

You Will Need:
- A shallow tray
- A jug of water
- A small mirror
- Modeling clay
- A friend
- A flashlight
- White cardstock

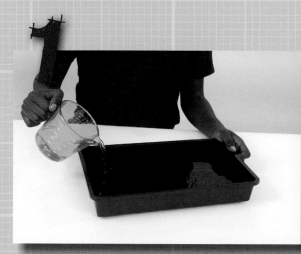

Step 1: Put the tray on a table or flat surface and pour in water to a depth of around 0.5 inches (1.25 cm).

Step 2: Rest the mirror inside the tray so that half of the mirror is underwater. Use the modeling clay to keep it in place, as shown above.

24

Step 3: Ask a friend to shine a flashlight at the mirror. At the same time, hold the white cardstock as a screen at the end opposite to the mirror.

Science Challenge

Step 4: Now you will need to figure out how to make a rainbow appear on the white screen. What happens when you shine the flashlight at the part of the mirror above the water? What happens when you shine the light at the part of the mirror that is under the water? You could try holding the white cardstock in different positions and the mirror at different angles. As you investigate, remember what you have learned about reflection and light traveling in straight lines.

Challenge Questions

- What did you do to make a rainbow form?
- Why did shining the flashlight at the part of the mirror underwater make a difference?
- Did angling the mirror and the cardstock make a difference?

INVESTIGATE MORE

Light is remarkable and important. The shadows, reflections, and refractions of light from different objects and materials give things we see shape and form, and help us experience the world around us. Light is also vitally useful in other ways, apart from seeing.

Light for Food and Power

Light energy helps green plants grow. Plant leaves capture light energy and use it to turn carbon dioxide in air and water into food, which the plant uses. When plants grow in the dark, they become pale and weak. In a similar way, light can be used to make power. Have you ever seen shiny solar panels on the roofs of buildings or on other objects, such as watches? Solar panels have layers of materials inside that can transform solar energy into electrical energy or power.

In the past, people on ships used patterns of flashes of light to send messages to other ships. Today, people send vast amounts of information between computers and cell phones using flashes of light through cables made of thin strands of glass. These cables are called optical fibers. The light is trapped in each optical fiber because it reflects back inward from the edges. Many animals, such as fireflies and squid, use light to send messages to each other, too!

Optical fibers carry vast amounts of information around the world in the form of light energy!

INVESTIGATE

What else would you like to discover about light? Telescopes use some of the biggest mirrors ever made. How do they work to help us see farther? Think about the convex lenses used in reading glasses. How could these relate to telescope mirrors? You could investigate some of the different ways we use light energy. **Laser** lights are used to cut metals and other materials, and to read and write DVDs. Some lasers are used in surgery to cut skin precisely. What other amazing uses of light energy can you find out about?

27

Science Challenge TIPS

Pages 12-13: Different Reflections

You should find that the greatest visibility of the object is when light is reflected off smooth foil, then white paper or crumpled foil, and finally, black paper. Black paper absorbs the most light, so it does not reflect a lot of light. The crumpled foil reflects light worse than smooth foil because the bumpy surface scatters reflected light. By keeping the flashlight at the same angle and the objects in the same position, your investigation will be more accurate and fair. Investigate further by using a brighter or dimmer flashlight. How do you think this would affect your results, and why?

Pages 18-19: Shadows

You should find that the farthest distance produces the sharpest silhouette. Up close, the flashlight throws a fuzzy shadow that is difficult to draw around. When you angle the flashlight from floor level, or above head height, the shadow can become unclear. That is because the light is closer to some parts than others. Make sure the light shining is from the same height as your friend's head.

You may spot a bigger difference in shadow size or sharpness if you try greater flashlight distances in a large darkened room. If your friend changes position, the test will no longer be fair and accurate.

Do you think adjusting the height of the flashlight would change the silhouette profile shape? Why? Explain your thinking.

Pages 24-25: Rainbows

You should be able to create or capture a rainbow of light on the white cardstock if you angle the cardstock and the flashlight just the right way. If it is not working, try aiming the flashlight beam at the part of the mirror under the water. When light hits the edge of the water, it is refracted and split into separate colors. When these light colors are reflected off the mirror, they are refracted again as they leave the water. You need to aim the flashlight beam and hold the white cardstock at the correct angle to ensure the reflected lights hit the cardstock so you can see the rainbow colors.

GLOSSARY

absorbed Soaked up

axis An imaginary line through the middle of something and around which it turns

angle The difference between the directions of two straight lines that meet

artificial Made by humans

bacteria Tiny living things too small to be seen with the naked eye

bioluminescence Light created naturally by living things such as fireflies

cells Tiny building blocks that make up all living things

convex A surface that curves or bulges outward

distorts Twists or pulls out of shape

energy Ability or power to do work

fluorescent Producing light when electricity flows through a tube that is filled with a type of gas

glare Strong, dazzling light

incandescence Light from heat

investigations Procedures carried out to observe, study, or test something to learn more about it

laser A narrow, powerful beam of light

lens The clear, curved part of the eye that focuses light on the retina at the back of the eye

lenses Artificial lenses are transparent, curved pieces of glass or plastic that refract (bend) light in useful ways, such as helping people see better

neon A gas that can be used in fluorescent lighting or signs

observe To use your senses to gather information

opaque Describes an object or surface that blocks light

prism A wedge of glass with triangular ends that splits light into its separate colors

pupil The tiny opening in the center of the iris, or the colored part of the eye, that appears to be black

reactions Processes in which two substances combine together chemically to form another substance

reflections Images that are reflected back at you by a very smooth and shiny surface, such as a mirror

reflects Bounces or throws back

refraction Bending of light

retina The area at the back of the eye that is sensitive to light and that can send signals to the brain to tell us what we are looking at

silhouette A dark shape or outline of an object set against a lighter background, often created by a shadow of an object in the sunshine

sources Places, people, or things from which something originates or can be obtained

spectrum The band of colors, as seen in a rainbow, produced when light is separated into its different colors

translucent Describes an object, surface, or material that lets some, but not all, light pass through it

transparent Describes an object, surface, or material that lets light pass through it

ultraviolet A type of invisible radiation that transfers heat energy

LEARNING MORE

Find out more about light and its uses.

Books

Canavan, Thomas. *Super Experiments With Light and Sound* (Mind-Blowing Science Experiments). Gareth Stevens, 2017.

DePrisco, Dorothea. *See for Yourself: The Ultimate Guide to Eyes.* Seagrass Press, 2017.

Hutchison, Patricia. *Focus on Light* (Hands-On STEM). North Star Editions, 2017.

Kenney, Karen Latchana. *Sound and Light Waves Investigations* (Key Questions in Physical Science). Lerner Publishing Group, 2017.

Websites

Discover more about the colors in light at:
http://idahoptv.org/sciencetrek/topics/light_and_color/facts.cfm

Read all about light at:
www.light2015.org/Home/LearnAboutLight.html

See how light reflects in different ways at:
www.optics4kids.org/home/content/what-is-optics/reflection/the-reflection-of-light

Learn about all kinds of aspects of light at:
www.sciencelearn.org.nz/resources/39-light-and-sight-introduction

INDEX

About the AUTHOR

Richard Spilsbury has a science degree, and has had a lifelong fascination with science. He has written and co-written many books for young people on a wide variety of topics, from ants to avalanches.

32